Reading for Success

Work and Play

PROGRAM AUTHORS
Richard L. Allington
Ronald L. Cramer
Patricia M. Cunningham
G. Yvonne Pérez
Constance Frazier Robinson
Robert J. Tierney

PROGRAM CONSULTANTS
Bernadine J. Bolden
Ann Hall
Sylvia M. Lee
Dolores Perez
Jo Ann Wong

CRITIC READERS
Maria P. Barela
Phinnize J. Brown
Jean C. Carter
Nancy Peterson
Nancy Welsh
Kay Williams

John C. Manning, *Instructional Consultant*

SCOTT, FORESMAN AND COMPANY
Editorial Offices: Glenview, Illinois

Regional Offices: Sunnyvale, California •
Tucker, Georgia • Glenview, Illinois •
Oakland, New Jersey • Dallas, Texas

ACKNOWLEDGMENTS

Text
"We Sang Songs" from *City Sun* by Eleanor Schick, Copyright ©
1974 by Eleanor Schick. Reprinted with permission of Macmillan
Publishing Co, Inc.

From *Another Here and Now Story Book* by Lucy Sprague Mitchell.
Copyright, 1937, E. P. Dutton & Co., Inc. Renewal, 1965, by
Lucy Sprague Mitchell. Reprinted by permission of the
publisher, E. P. Dutton, Inc.

Artists
Brooks, Nan: Pages 28–29;
Connelly, Gwen: Pages 6–7, 8–15, 18–27, 30–47, 58–61;
Iosa, Ann: Pages 16–17, 48–57; Masheris, Robert: Pages 62–63

Cover Artist
Gwen Connelly

Contents

Section Page   5   Section

Unit 1   ◆ 6   Fun in School

          8   The 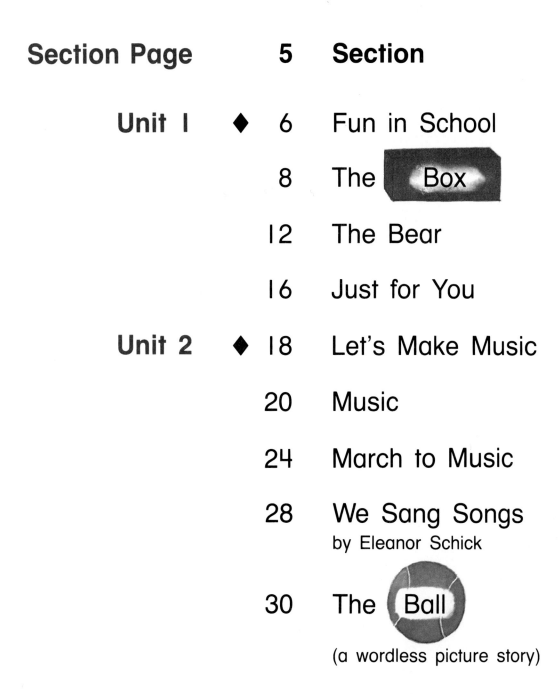 Box

        12   The Bear

        16   Just for You

Unit 2   ◆ 18   Let's Make Music

        20   Music

        24   March to Music

        28   We Sang Songs
                 by Eleanor Schick

        30   The Ball
                 (a wordless picture story)

Unit 3 ◆ 34   Who Likes the Sun?

36   The Sun, The Rain

41   Blue Rain, Yellow Sun

Unit 4 ◆ 46   Books to Read

48   Who Likes Books?

53   A Green House for a Bear

58   A Mouse in a House

62   The House of the Mouse
by Lucy Sprague Mitchell

64   Word List

Stories by: Katy Hall

Work and Play

Fun in School

The **Box**

The boy has a box .

David sees the  box .

Pat sees the  box .

The boy has a bear.

David likes the bear.

Pat likes the bear.

The bear likes David.

The bear likes Pat.

The Bear

Ben has a bear.

David likes the bear.

Pat likes the bear.

Pat makes a big bear.

Pat makes a  cap for the big bear.

Pat makes the big bear for David.

David makes a big bear.

David makes a kite for the big bear.

David makes the big bear for Pat.

Ben has a bear.

David has a bear.

Pat has a bear.

Let's Make Music

Music

Ben sees the 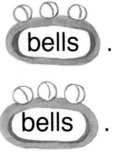 bells .

Ben likes the bells .

Ben plays the bells .

Ben plays music for David.

Ben plays music for Pat.

David sees the big  .

David likes the big 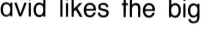 .

Pat sees the big  .

Pat likes the big  .

David has the big  drum .

David plays music.

Pat plays the big  drum .

Pat plays music.

March to Music

David likes to march.

Pat likes to march.

Ben likes to march.

David plays a horn.

David plays music.

Pat plays a drum.

Pat plays music.

Ben plays the (bells).

Ben plays music.

The girl likes the music.

David likes to march.

Pat likes to march.

Ben likes to march.

The girl likes to march!

To be read by the teacher

We Sang Songs

by Eleanor Schick

We sang songs
in school
all afternoon,
and now
my shoes
are singing
them back
to me.

The Ball

Who Likes the Sun?

The Sun, The Rain

Who sees the yellow sun?

David sees the yellow sun.

David likes the yellow sun.

Who sees the  seal ?

Pat sees the seal .

Pat likes the seal .

Who sees the  monkey ?

Laura sees the  monkey .

Laura likes the  monkey .

Pat sees the  seal .

David sees the yellow sun.

Laura sees the monkey .

Who sees the 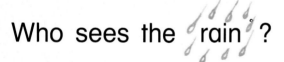rain?

David!

Pat!

Laura!

Who likes the rain?

Blue Rain, Yellow Sun

Who likes the rain?

Ben likes the rain.

Ben has some blue paint.

Ben makes some blue rain.

Who has some blue paint?

Ben has some blue paint.

Ben makes a big blue 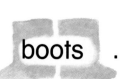 hat .

Ben makes big blue boots .

Who likes the sun?

David likes the sun.

David has some yellow paint.

David makes a yellow sun.

Who has some yellow paint?

David has some yellow paint.

David makes a yellow hat .

David makes big yellow boots .

Who likes the blue rain ?

Ben likes the blue rain .

Who likes the yellow sun?

David likes the yellow sun.

Books to Read

Who Likes Books?

Big Bear has a book.

Big Bear likes the book.

Big Bear plays.

Big Bear likes big blue books.

Big Bear likes little blue books.

Big Bear likes big yellow books.

Big Bear likes little yellow books.

Little Bear has a book.

Little Bear likes to read.

Little Bear likes to read the book.

Little Bear sees Big Bear.

Little Bear sees the books.

Who likes to read books?

Little Bear likes to read books.

Big Bear likes to read books.

A Green House for a Bear

The bear can read a book.

The bear sees a big green

house in the book.

The bear sees a little green

house in the book.

The bear likes green houses.

The bear has a little house.

The bear has some paint.

Can the bear paint the

little house green?

The bear has some blue paint.

The bear has some yellow paint.

The bear makes some green paint.

The bear makes some green paint in

a big  pail .

The bear can paint the roof green.

The bear can paint the door green.

The bear can paint the

little house green.

The bear likes green houses.

The bear likes to read books.

The bear can read in the

little green house.

The bear can read books in the

little green house.

A Mouse in a House

Laura makes a blue house for

a 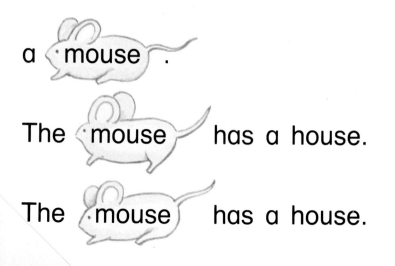 mouse .

The mouse has a house.

The mouse has a house.

David makes a little yellow house

for a  mouse .

The mouse has a house.

The mouse has a house.

The 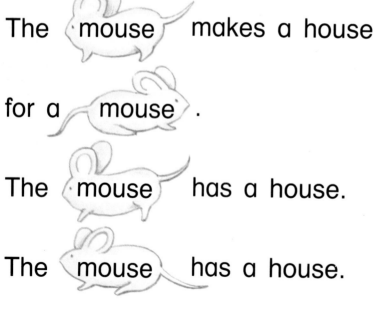 mouse makes a house

for a mouse .

The mouse has a house.

The mouse has a house.

The  mouse likes the house!

The House of the Mouse

by Lucy Sprague Mitchell

The house of the mouse
is a wee little house,
a green little house in the grass,
which big clumsy folk
may hunt and may poke
and still never see as they pass

this sweet little, neat little,
wee little, green little,
cuddle-down hide-away
house in the grass.

Word Lists

The words below are listed by unit. Following each word is the page of first appearance of the word.

Unit 1, 6-17

has 8

bear 10

big 13

for 13

Unit 2, 18-33

music 20

plays 21

march 24

to 24

Unit 3, 34-45

sun 36

who 36

yellow 36

blue 41

some 41

paint 41

Unit 4, 46-63

book 48

little 49

read 50

green 53

house 53

can 53

in 53